AF588311

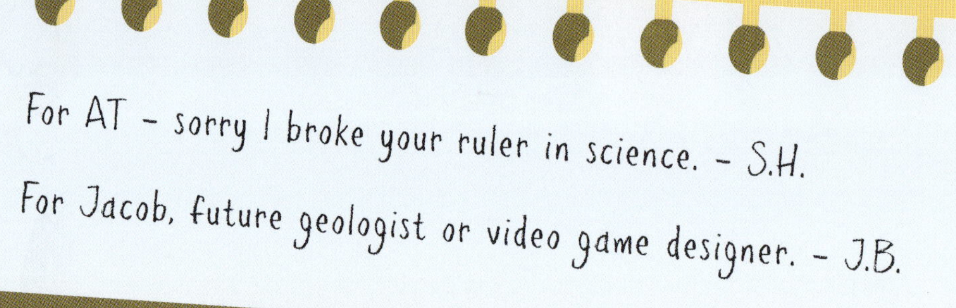


First published in Great Britain 2026 by Red Shed, part of Farshore
An imprint of HarperCollins*Publishers*
1 London Bridge Street,
London SE1 9GF
www.farshore.co.uk

HarperCollins*Publishers*
Macken House, 39/40 Mayor Street Upper
Dublin 1, D01 C9W8, Ireland

Red Shed is a registered trademark of HarperCollins*Publishers* Ltd.


Consultancy by Jules Pottle and Dr Patricia Macnair.

ISBN 978 0 00 871337 9
Printed in Malaysia.
1

A CIP catalogue record for this title is available from the British Library.



Stay safe online. Any website addresses listed in this book are correct at the time of going to print. However, Farshore is not responsible for content hosted by third parties. Please be aware that online content can be subject to change and websites can contain content that is unsuitable for children. We advise that all children are supervised when using the internet.

Experiments and activities are performed at your own risk, follow the instructions and ALWAYS ask an adult for help. HarperCollins is not responsible for the results of your experiments. Always ask an adult for help with any craft activity or DIY project. Wear protective clothes and cover surfaces to avoid damage or staining.

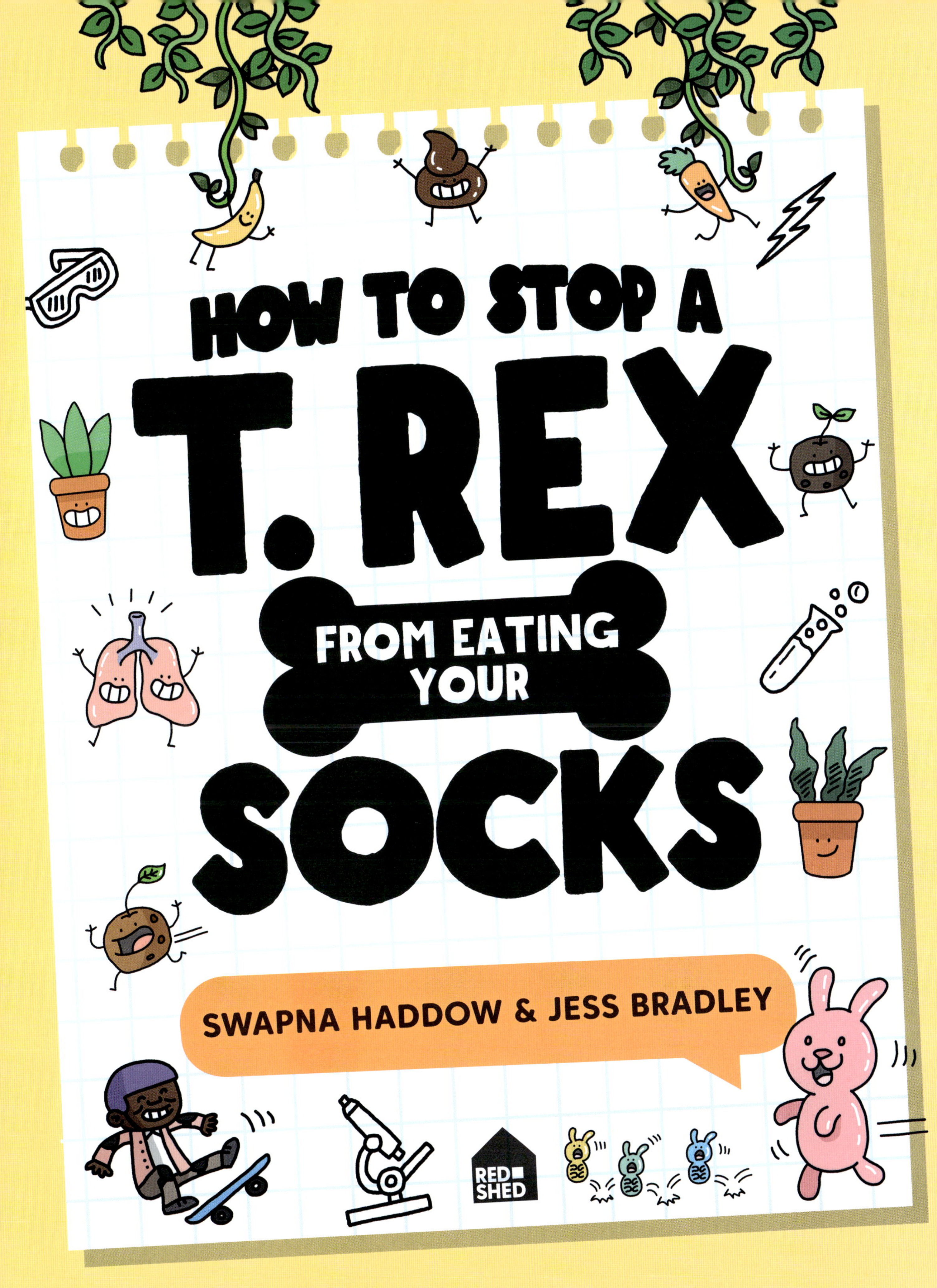
HOW TO STOP A
T. REX
FROM EATING YOUR
SOCKS
SWAPNA HADDOW & JESS BRADLEY
RED SHED

# INTRODUCTION

The bonkers world of science has some of the answers to how things work and why things don't. In this book, you will find ridiculous and not-so-ridiculous dilemmas, which all have solutions from the astonishing and unbelievable world of science. All the hard work has been done for you - thanks to fantastic scientists - but you can test out the science for yourself with an experiment at the end of each section.

Many scientists have made amazing discoveries from trying out experiments. Just take Jewel Plummer Cobb, an American biologist. Her experiments helped improve the understanding and treatment of skin cancer - she was also a brilliant advocate for women of colour in science!

You'll come away with all the knowledge you need to survive everything - including a trip to Mars and meeting a hungry T. rex.

**Pssst!**

The brilliant thing about science is that even if it doesn't go the way you expect, you've still learned something. You've learned that it doesn't work. The magic of learning through science is that it is all about experimenting and discovering. **JUST MAKE SURE THAT YOU'VE CHECKED WITH A PARENT OR GUARDIAN BEFORE YOU START!** (They can also help with any tricky bits AND you can wow them with your new knowledge!)

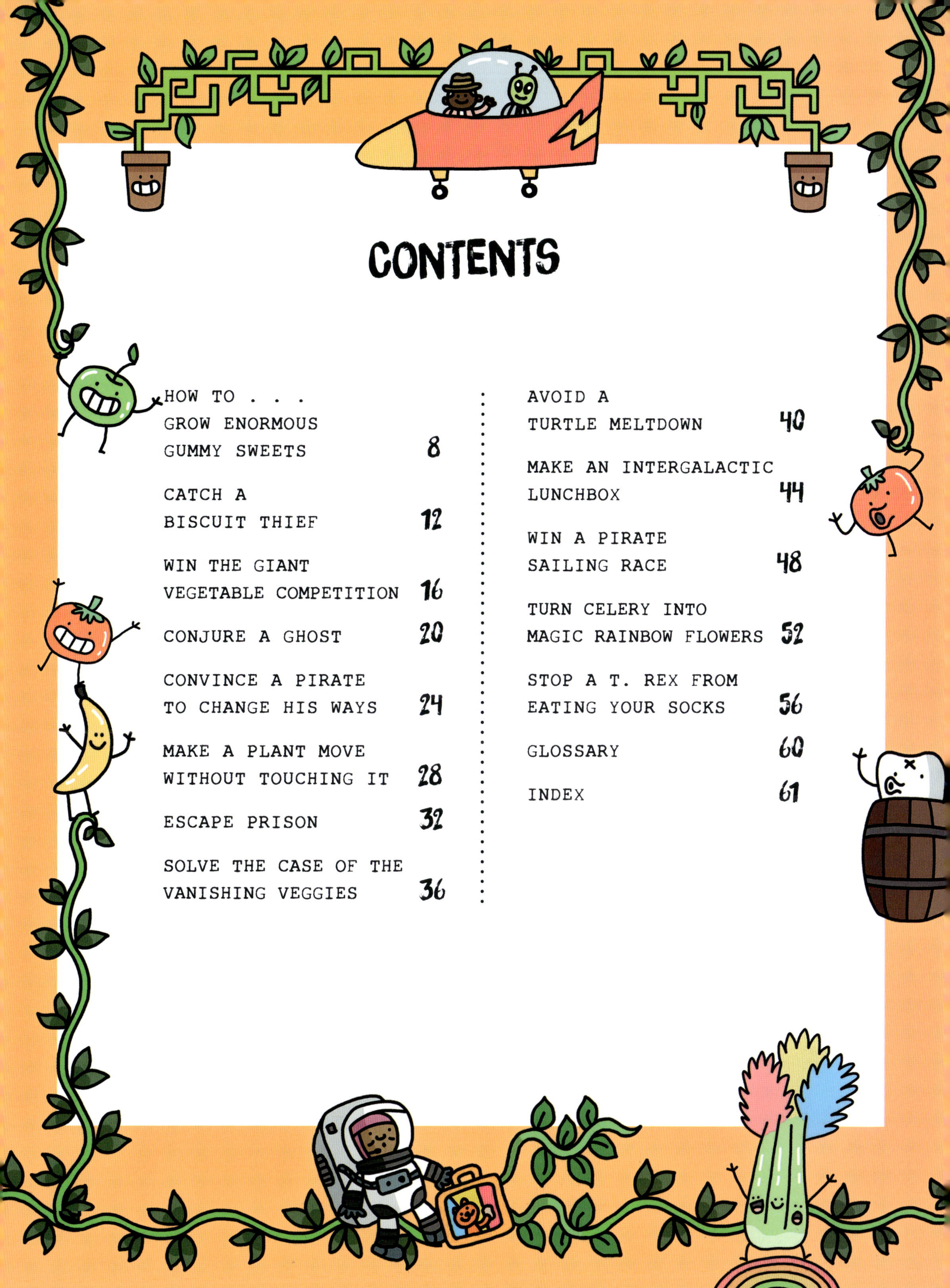

# CONTENTS

**CALAMITY COMICS** 1

# HOW TO GROW ENORMOUS GUMMY SWEETS

*THE SCIENCE COMIC YOU NEVER KNEW YOU NEEDED* | BIOLOGY EDITION

Archie, Archie's grandad, Zoe and Ava are at the skatepark practising their tricks. Everyone has brought snacks to share afterwards and Archie has brought his favourite gummy sweets. But – disaster!

Grandad knocked Archie's sweets off the table mid kickflip . . .

. . . and into a giant puddle!

Luckily, two sweets had fallen out in Archie's pocket earlier.

But how can he share these out?

What do YOU think Archie should do . . .

A) BORROW A WATER BOTTLE?

B) EAT THE SWEETS HIMSELF?

C) SEARCH HIS POCKETS FOR MORE SWEETS?

If you chose **A**, AWESOME CHOICE! Archie can use the magic of how cells work to grow his gummy bears to share with everyone.
If you chose **B**, Archie feels terrible after, especially as Ava and Zoe shared their sweets with him last week.
If you chose **C**, this is hopeless. All he finds is a dusty pen lid.

Turn the book upside down to see the answers!

## WHAT'S THE SCIENCE?

Did you know that all living things are made of **cells**? Cells are tiny units a bit like building blocks. There are around 37 trillion cells in the human body, including blood cells, bone cells and skin cells.

Each cell has a **cell membrane** - a layer around the edge. It's strong enough to hold the cell together, but can let water through to keep the cell healthy. The process of water moving in and out of cells is called **osmosis**. Water likes to flow through membranes when there is less water on the other side. When there are equal amounts of water on both sides of the membrane, less movement happens.

Let's take a closer look at osmosis in action to see how it might help Archie.

# SEE OSMOSIS IN ACTION

The sugar-rich jelly in gummy sweets works a bit like the cells in our bodies. The outside of the sweet is solid but can let water through.

## You will need:

- A gummy sweet*
- A ruler
- A pencil
- Paper
- Water
- A measuring jug
- A bowl

*Be careful – don't eat the sweet after the experiment, in case bacteria has formed.

## Instructions:

1. Measure your sweet and write down the length.

2. Add water to the bowl (just enough to cover the sweet).

3. Place the sweet in the bowl and leave it overnight.

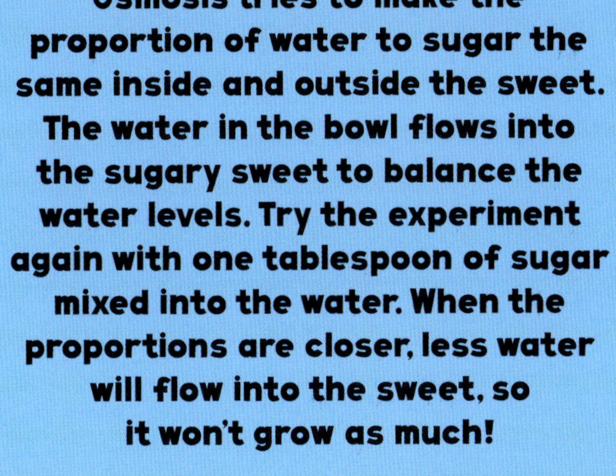

4. Take out the sweet and measure it again. Note down the size – what has happened?

If Archie pops the two sweets into a water bottle and waits for long enough, the water will travel into the sweets through osmosis until they are ginormous (or at least a bit bigger). Archie just needs to steer clear of his grandad's water bottle, which has orange squash in it - the sugar in the squash will mean the sweets won't grow as big. The friends shouldn't eat the giant sweets in case any bacteria has formed - but they all give Archie top marks for his science skills!

## CALAMITY COMICS

2

# HOW TO CATCH A BISCUIT THIEF

*THE SCIENCE COMIC YOU NEVER KNEW YOU NEEDED* | BIOLOGY EDITION

Yawn! Amy has spent the whole morning trudging around the supermarket, helping her mum with the weekly big shop. It's Amy's least favourite chore of the week . . . but once the shopping is put away, Amy can treat herself to a biscuit or two.

Amy had chosen the double chocolate chip biscuits with extra chocolateyness.

HOLD ON! Where have those biscuits gone? There's a thief in the house!

Are those crumbs round Granny's mouth?

Is that chocolate on Dad's cheek?

Amy is ON THE CASE.

Should Amy . . .

A) ACCUSE BOTH OF THEM?

B) GO BACK TO THE SHOP?

C) BRING OUT THE MARSHMALLOWS?

If you chose **A**, this is a disaster. Dad and Granny deny eating the biscuits.

If you chose **B**, Amy's mum decides she can't face another trip to the supermarket, so Amy has to go without biscuits.

If you chose **C**, WELL DONE! Marshmallows will help reveal who has been running to steal the sweet treats.

## WHAT'S THE SCIENCE?

Understanding the amazing human body will be helpful here. **Muscles** are attached to bones in the body and help move it in different ways. Muscles need oxygen and **nutrients** to work. Luckily, the human body has a speedy delivery system to get this fuel to them: blood. Blood gets transported around the body through a network of blood vessels (veins, arteries and capillaries).

One way to feel the blood moving round your body is by gently presssing a finger onto your wrist just under the bottom of your thumb. You'll notice a bouncy knocking - your **pulse**! This shows how fast your heart is pumping. The heart is constantly delivering oxygen-rich blood to the muscles, but it pumps faster during exercise. This fact will help Amy . . .

Turn the page to find out how.

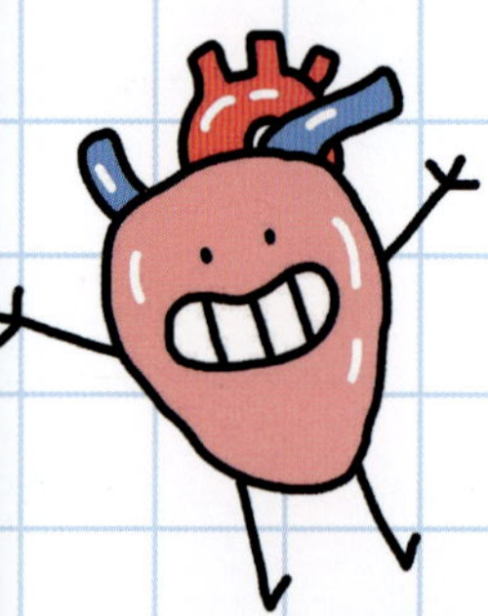

# MAKE A MODEL HEART

Experiment by making your own pump – the heart pumps blood in a similar way!

**You will need:**

- A glass jar
- Water
- A balloon
- Scissors*
- Two paper straws
- Sticky tape

*Be careful – ask an adult for help.

**Try this experiment on a surface you can wipe clean and that you don't mind getting wet!**

**Instructions:**

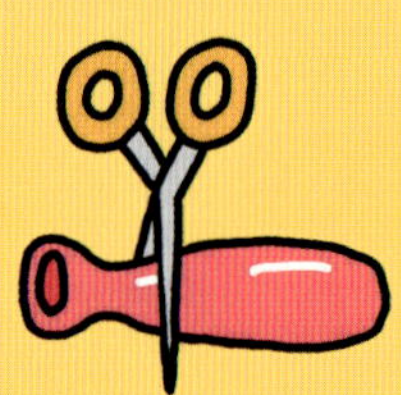

1. Half-fill the jar with water. Ask an adult to cut the end off the balloon and stretch it over the top of the jar like a lid.

2. Ask an adult to cut two small holes in the stretched balloon (use tape to make them smaller if needed). Push the straws in so the ends go under the water.

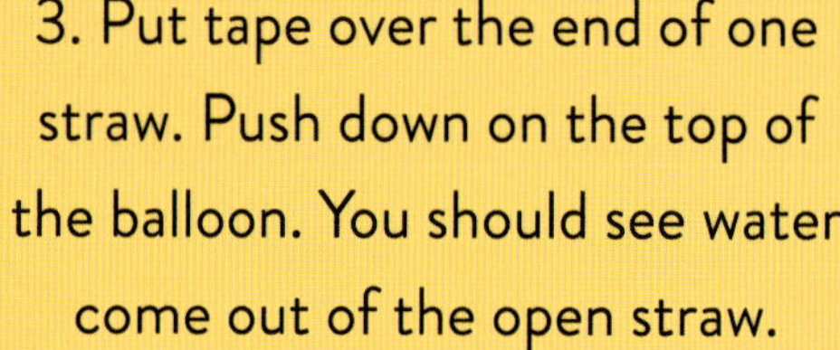

3. Put tape over the end of one straw. Push down on the top of the balloon. You should see water come out of the open straw.

# MAKE A PULSE DETECTOR

This is a fun activity to see how our pulse changes before and after exercise. And there's a tasty treat for afters!

**You will need:**

- A mini marshmallow
- A toothpick*

*Be careful – ask an adult for help.

**Don't worry if your pulse isn't very strong – it can vary in different people. If you can't see much happening, try the experiment out on some friends and family!**

**Instructions:**

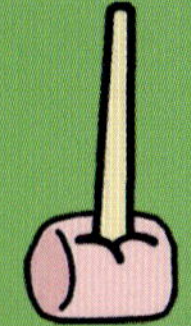

1. Ask an adult to help you poke the toothpick into the marshmallow.

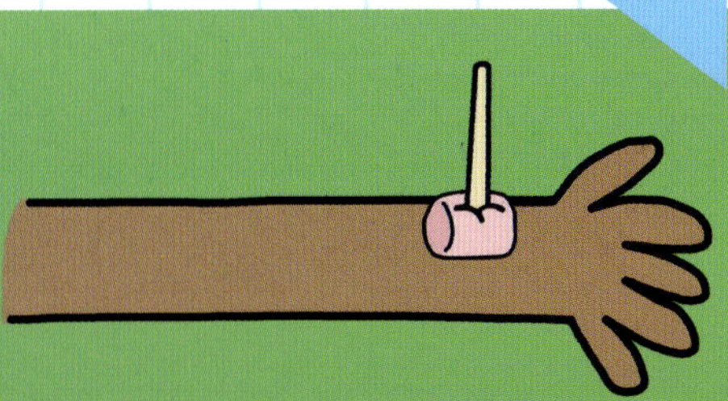

2. Lay your arm on a table. Place the marshmallow on your wrist.

3. Watch as your pulse makes the marshmallow jiggle! Cool, eh?

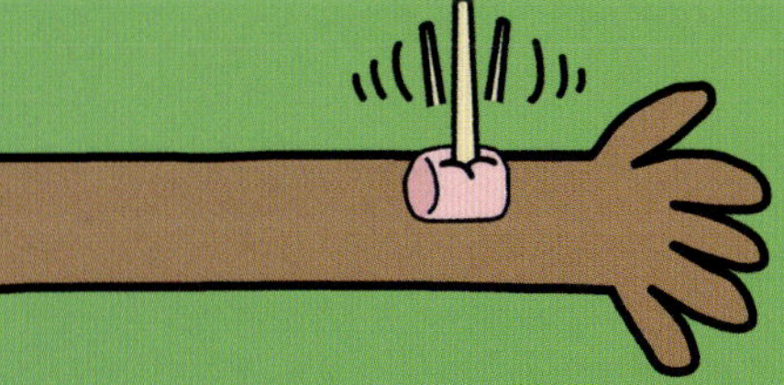

4. Do 20 star jumps, then try again. Your pulse will be quicker . . . meaning faster marshmallow jiggling!

If Amy is quick enough and measures the two suspects' pulses straight after the theft, she will see that her dad's is very quick. Almost as if he ran straight to find the freshly unpacked biscuits. He crumbles, just like the biscuits he munched. Case closed!

# CALAMITY COMICS

3

# HOW TO WIN THE GIANT VEGETABLE COMPETITION

*THE SCIENCE COMIC YOU NEVER KNEW YOU NEEDED* | BIOLOGY EDITION

Rocky and Flynn are entering their school's enormous vegetable competition! Last year, Anika won first prize with a courgette the size of a small dog, and she's been busy in her greenhouse all summer looking after an onion the size of her head. It's going to be a tough competition.

Rocky and Flynn have decided on something spectacular – a pumpkin! But where to grow a prize-winning one?

Rocky thinks they should grow it in the container by their house.

Flynn thinks the best spot is by the school shed. How can they make sure they win?

**Should Rocky and Flynn . . .**

A) HIDE ANIKA'S ONION?

B) GRAB SOME PANTS AND A JAR?

C) GROW TWO PUMPKINS?

If you chose **A**, Anika is no fool. She finds the onion in Flynn's sock drawer immediately, and Rocky and Flynn are disqualified from the competition.

If you chose **B**, AWESOME IDEA! Rocky and Flynn can use the pants to test the soil quality and choose the best spot based on SCIENCE.

If you chose **C**, oops. Rocky and Flynn spend so much time going between the two places that neither of the pumpkins get enough water and they end up teeny-tiny.

## WHAT'S THE SCIENCE?

Soil is brilliant for plants. It holds water and nutrients for growth and helps keep their **roots** in place. Different plants often need different types of soil with different nutrients in it. Pumpkins like lots of organic matter in their soil - compost, for example. This is made from materials, such as food scraps and leaves, that have been left to rot into a nutritious mixture.

Healthy soil has many microbes (tiny living things that can be seen only with a microscope). It also has larger decomposers, such as earthworms and flies. These creatures feed on carbon-rich materials, such as compost. Their digestion process releases useful nutrients, often in their poo!

Helpfully for Rocky and Flynn, pants are another carbon-rich material. Let's try some experiments!

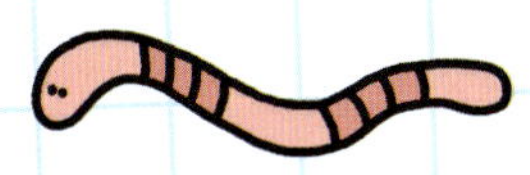

# TEST YOUR SOIL

This experiment takes a bit of patience, but is a great and easy way to test soil quality. Try it out in a couple of places to compare!

**You will need:**

- Old, 100 per cent cotton pants
- A spade or a trowel*
- A stick

*Be careful – ask an adult for help.

**Try checking on the pants every few weeks to see the process in action!**

**Instructions:**

1. Find a patch of soil to test and ask an adult to help you dig a small hole.

2. Place the pants in the hole and cover them with soil. Put your stick on top to mark the spot.

3. This is where patience is needed – wait for a couple of months, then dig up the pants. Healthy soil has lots of carbon-eating microbes . . . so pants left in healthy soil will be very nibbled!

# DISCOVER SOIL LAYERS

Plants love to grow in soil that has lots of organic matter, called 'humus'. (Not the houmous you might eat with carrots!) Here's an easy way to see the different materials in soil - and check how much humus is in it.

**You will need:**

- A couple of handfuls of soil
- A glass jar with a lid
- Water
- A spoon

**Sand and stones sink to the bottom because they are the heaviest materials. A slightly lighter layer, called silt, sits on top of the sand. On top of that is clay, which is lighter again. Humus sits at the top.**

**Instructions:**

1. Put the soil into the jar and fill it nearly to the top with water.

2. Stir, then put on the lid and leave for 2–3 hours.

3. Look at the different layers!

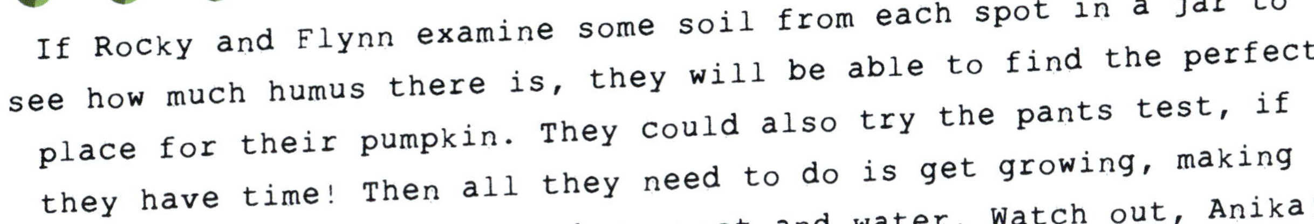

If Rocky and Flynn examine some soil from each spot in a jar to see how much humus there is, they will be able to find the perfect place for their pumpkin. They could also try the pants test, if they have time! Then all they need to do is get growing, making sure their pumpkin has enough compost and water. Watch out, Anika!

## CALAMITY COMICS

4

# HOW TO CONJURE A GHOST

*THE SCIENCE COMIC YOU NEVER KNEW YOU NEEDED* — *BIOLOGY EDITION*

It's Halloween and Ava and Zoe's spooky tricks have reached an all-time high. Ava says she's read all the scary books and been on every funfair ghost train that has ever come to town. She claims she is the Halloween Champion. Can Zoe prove Ava wrong?

Last year, Zoe jumped out at her best friend . . .

But Ava wasn't spooked in the slightest.

Then Zoe found A HAND in her lunchbox!

It was a fake one from Ava, covered in ketchup.

It's time for Zoe to step up her game.

Should Zoe . . .

A) USE AVA TO SPOOK AVA?

B) TRY JUMPING OUT AT AVA AGAIN?

C) ACCEPT AVA'S THE HALLOWEEN CHAMPION?

If you chose **A**, AWESOME IDEA! Zoe can use the science of our brains to get Ava to scare herself.

If you chose **B**, this doesn't work. Eagle-eyed Ava sees Zoe coming.

If you chose **C**, no way! Zoe is not a quitter.

## WHAT'S THE SCIENCE?

Did you know that sitting in your head right now is a supercomputer? That's right – it's your brain!

Not only are our brains in charge of everything from thinking to breathing, they can predict things too. If a ball flies towards your head, you duck without thinking. Your brain predicts that the ball will hit you, so it sends super-fast signals to your muscles to move your head out of the way.

Sometimes, though, our eyes can trick our brains – this is called an optical illusion. Information from our eyes travels to the brain through **neurons**, special cells that act like messengers. If there are any gaps in the information, the brain tries to fill these in. But sometimes, the brain doesn't get it quite right.

Turn over for a spooky experiment . . .

# MAKE A GHOST APPEAR

Feeling brave? This spooky experiment is a great way to see the mysterious and incredible things your brain can do.

**You will need:**

- A dimly lit room
- A mirror
- A timer

**Instructions:**

1. Find a mirror in a dimly lit room that you can comfortably look at yourself in.

2. Set your timer for 2–3 minutes. Then stare at your face, keeping your expression neutral. Don't look away!

3. After a few minutes, you'll start to see your features changing – a bit ghost-like!

4. If this doesn't happen, try making your surroundings even darker then try again.

**Wahhh! What was that? Don't worry, take a breath, it's not a ghost. The strange face appears because of something called the Troxler effect. When your brain looks at something that doesn't change for a long time, it starts to ignore the unchanging parts. This means you start seeing things that aren't really there!**

If Zoe sets up a mirror in a dimly lit room and convinces Ava to stare at herself, Ava will see a seriously spooky sight – and Zoe can become the Halloween Champion!

CALAMITY COMICS

5

# HOW TO CONVINCE A PIRATE TO CHANGE HIS WAYS

THE SCIENCE COMIC YOU NEVER KNEW YOU NEEDED | BIOLOGY EDITION

Amy has brought a bunch of pirates in to school to help her with Show and Tell. Captain Rottenleg and his crew are heading into the classroom but the captain looks in pain . . .

Rottenleg has toothache! He says that he hasn't brushed his teeth for days . . .

. . . but he's sure his favourite orange juice will help!

Amy knows this is a bad idea because of what her dentist told her.

How can Amy show Rottenleg what's happening to his teeth?

Should Amy . . .

A) GO AND FIND AN EGG?

B) GIVE THE CAPTAIN HIS ORANGE JUICE?

C) DO A SHOW AND TELL ALL ABOUT TEETH?

If you chose **A**, HOORAY! A quick 'eggs-periment' will show Rottenleg that drinking acidic, sugary juice and not brushing his teeth is causing his toothache. If you chose **B**, Rottenleg will learn that the juice isn't helping him . . . but only because his teeth will hurt even more. Grumpy pirate ahoy! If you chose **C**, good idea . . . but unfortunately Rottenleg wasn't listening - he was looting beanbags from the PE cupboard instead.

## WHAT'S THE SCIENCE?

Teeth help us to break down our food. There are different kinds - adults have incisors, canines, molars, premolars and wisdom teeth - each with a specific job, such as chewing or biting. They are kept in place by the gums, the pinkish bit that you see in the mirror when you give yourself a big toothy grin.

You've probably heard this a gazillion times, but it's important to look after your teeth. Unlike bull sharks, who have up to 50 rows of teeth that get constantly replaced, we only have two sets - baby teeth and adult teeth. It's important to brush twice a day and floss at least once a day. Unfortunately, Captain Rottenleg didn't follow this advice! A combination of not brushing and drinking a lot of sugary, acidic juice has damaged his teeth.

Let's take a closer look . . .

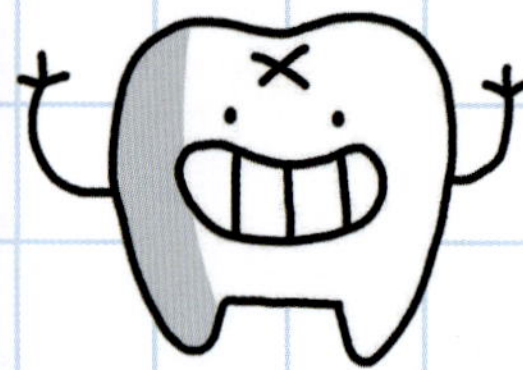

# MAKE 'TEETH' ROT

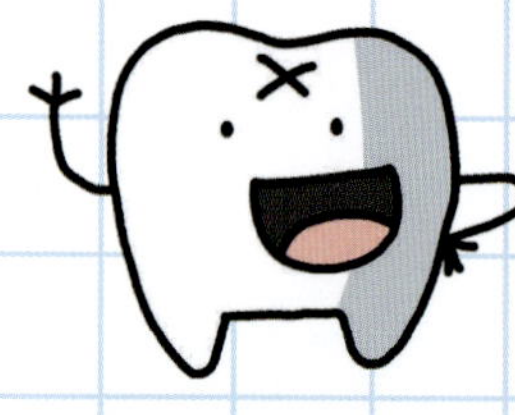

Don't worry, we're going to use eggshells as 'teeth' rather than your own! This is a great way to see what acid and sugar in our food does to teeth in our mouth.

## You will need:

- Two hard boiled eggs in their shells*
- Two glasses
- Some orange juice
- Water

*Be careful – ask an adult to boil the eggs for you, and wait until they cool down.

**Orange juice is good for your body in small quantities, but not good for your teeth. Dentists advise drinking juice quickly with a meal so it doesn't linger on your teeth. Wait for one hour before brushing to avoid damaging the enamel.**

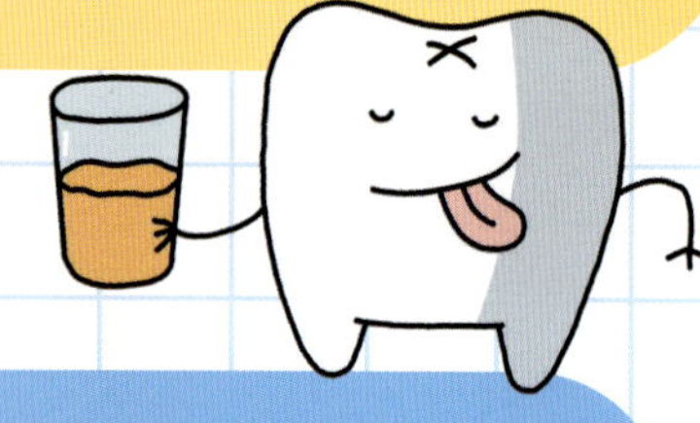

## Instructions:

1. Carefully place an egg in each glass.

2. Fully cover one egg with orange juice.

3. Fully cover the other egg with water.

4. Place both glasses in the fridge.

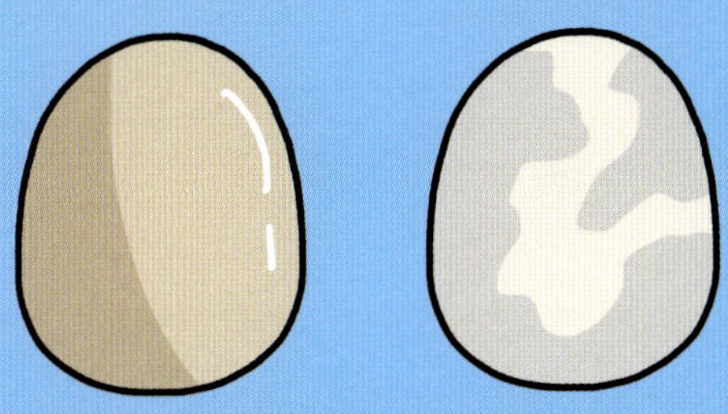

5. Leave the eggs for 2–3 days, then carefully take them out of the liquid. What do you notice?

**Water doesn't change the eggshell, but the orange juice makes it softer if left for a long time. That's what happens to our teeth! Food and drinks with a lot of sugar and acid can damage the outer layer of teeth (enamel) over time, exposing the soft layers beneath (dentine and pulp). This can cause a horrid toothache!**

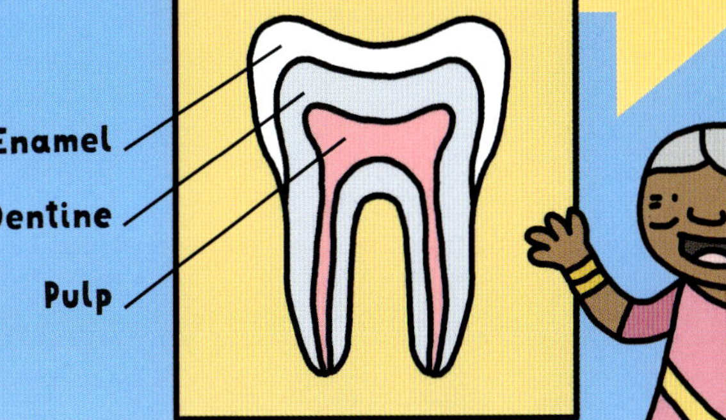


If Amy fetches an egg, leaves it in some of Rottenleg's juice for a while and shows him the results, she could help him understand why he's got a toothache. He'll be off to the dentist in no time to get some fillings done. Rottenleg will also brush twice a day from now on and have his orange juice in small quantities as a special treat. A pirate has treasure to hunt for and Show and Tells to attend, so needs to keep healthy!

CALAMITY COMICS

6

# HOW TO MAKE A PLANT MOVE WITHOUT TOUCHING IT

THE SCIENCE COMIC YOU NEVER KNEW YOU NEEDED

BIOLOGY EDITION

Amy has a big sleepover planned. She's going to have a movie night with her friends and the popcorn is ready to go! There's just one problem . . . Granny has left her prize plant in front of the TV.

Amy's been told not to touch Granny's plant – in any circumstances!

But they can't watch the movie through the leaves.

How can Amy rescue the sleepover before it's too late?

**Should Amy . . .**

A) MOVE THE PLANT?

B) WATCH THE PLANT INSTEAD OF A MOVIE?

C) GRAB A BOX?

If you chose **A**, oops. When Granny finds out, Amy's in BIG trouble!
If you chose **B**, bad idea. Amy's friends wanted excitement and suspense, and the plant is just not delivering. Everyone ends up going to sleep early. Boring!
If you chose **C**, BRILLIANT idea. By using a box, Amy can use science to move the plant without touching it.

# WHAT'S THE SCIENCE?

Have you ever noticed how a plant grows towards the Sun? Try looking at one - you might see their leaves reaching towards the light.

Plants love light - it's the main energy source in a process called **photosynthesis**, that plants use to make the food and energy they need to grow. Plants take light from the Sun, water from the ground and **carbon dioxide** from the air, and transform all three into energy.

Plants also contain **auxin**. This builds up on the shady side of the plant, making that side more stretchy, so it can bend more. This helps the plant grow towards the light it needs - and even get around obstacles!

Ready to try an experiment to help Amy?

# PLANT A MAZE

Have a go at transforming plants into amazing shapes using the power of light!

## You will need:

- A seed from a fast-growing plant (e.g. a bean)
- A few handfuls of soil
- Water
- A plant pot
- A shoebox
- Scissors*
- A sheet of thick, black paper or card
- Sticky tape

*Be careful – ask an adult for help.

If your seed doesn't sprout, don't give up! Start again with a new seed.

## Instructions:

1. Fill the pot with soil and moisten with water. Plant the seed.

2. Leave the pot in a light place, adding a little water each day. After around 3–6 days, you'll notice a sprout emerging.

3. Make the maze. Ask an adult to cut a hole on the left side of one of the short edges of the shoebox.

4. Ask an adult to cut the card or paper to make a divider for the middle of the box. Cut a hole on one side.

5. Tape the divider in place in the box. Place your plant under the divider, then put the lid back on.

6. Place the box in a light place. Take the lid off and give your plant a little water each day.

7. Watch how it grows through the box towards the light!

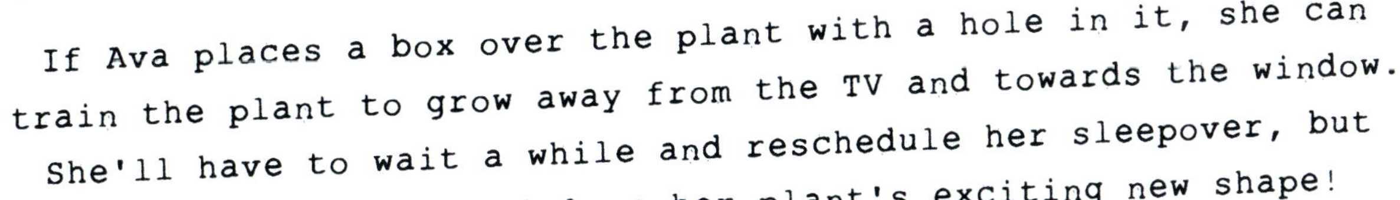

If Ava places a box over the plant with a hole in it, she can train the plant to grow away from the TV and towards the window. She'll have to wait a while and reschedule her sleepover, but hopefully Granny will love her plant's exciting new shape!

# CALAMITY COMICS

# HOW TO ESCAPE PRISON

7

THE SCIENCE COMIC YOU NEVER KNEW YOU NEEDED | BIOLOGY EDITION

Anika's dad is a tour guide at the city's police station museum. He was getting ready for Anika's class to visit when he accidently locked himself in the holding cell exhibit. This is very embarrassing . . . because it's the second time it has happened.

He had found some craft supplies for the class to make paper police hats.

He went into the holding cell to turn on the light . . .

. . . when the door clanged shut behind him! The key is just out of reach outside. How can he reach it before the class arrives?

**Should Anika's dad . . .**

A) SAY SOMEONE LOCKED HIM IN?

B) RUMMAGE IN THE CRAFT BOX?

C) PRETEND HE'S PART OF THE DISPLAY?

If you chose **A**, this backfires spectacularly. A full investigation is launched, revealing that Anika's dad did indeed lock himself in.

If you chose **B**, BRILLIANT choice! By using card, straws and string, he can make himself a 'hand' to reach the keys.

If you chose **C**, big mistake. Anika recognises him straight away!

# WHAT'S THE SCIENCE?

Our **skeleton** is made of bones – they work together with muscles to help us do incredible things, like cartwheels.

Muscles are attached to bones with flexible cords called tendons. Safely fixed in place, muscles can move different body parts. They often work together as a pair, or in groups, to move the bones in different directions by one muscle contracting (tightening) as the other relaxes.

Bones can't bend, but they are cleverly held together at the **joints**, such as elbows, knees, wrists and knuckles. These let the body move in different directions.

Let's try an experiment to take a closer look at how brilliant skeletons are.

# MAKE A HAND

Hands can do everything from guiding a pencil and drawing, to gently stroking the top of a hamster's head. Let's have a look at how they work.

## You will need:

- A piece of thick paper
- A pencil
- Scissors*
- A packet of paper straws
- String (five pieces about the length of your hand
- Sticky tape

*Be careful – ask an adult for help.

**In real life, tendons attach to the outside of our bones rather than going through the middle.**

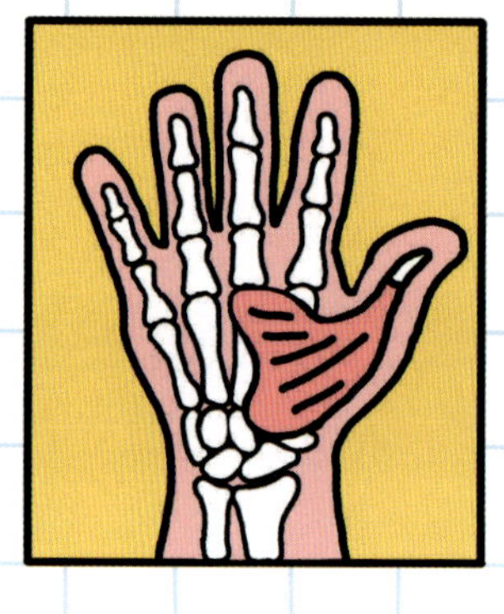

## Instructions:

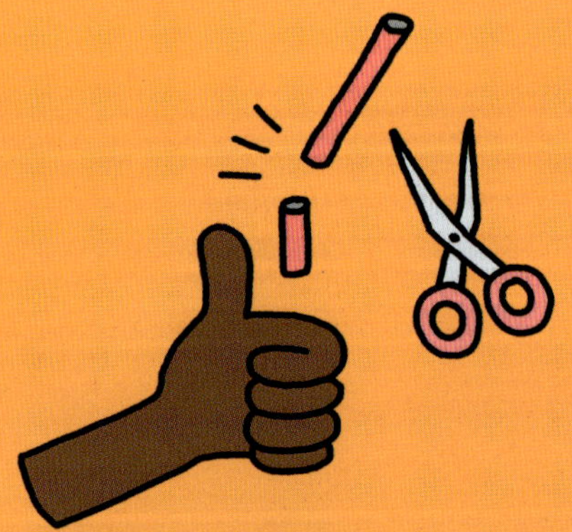

1. Draw around your hand on the paper. Ask an adult to help you cut it out.

2. Ask an adult to help you cut straws into pieces that match the different bones in your fingers and thumb, between your joints.

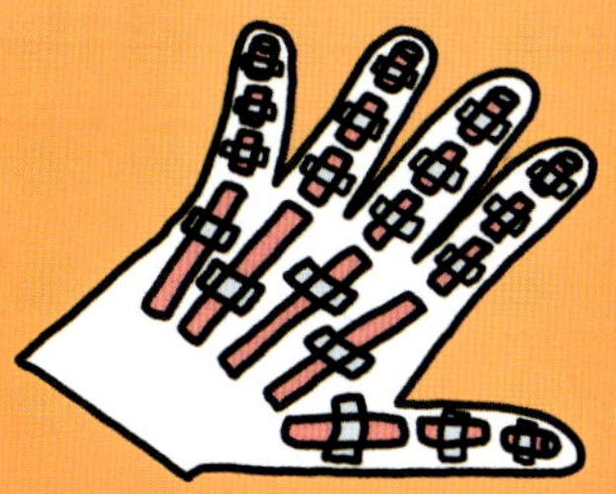

3. Tape pieces of straw onto the paper fingers, matching the positions from your own fingers.

4. Cut five lengths of straw to match the bones running from your wrist to the bottom of your fingers and thumb. Tape in place.

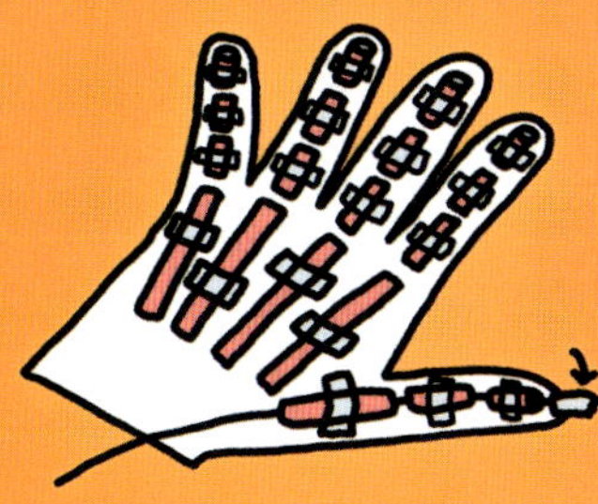

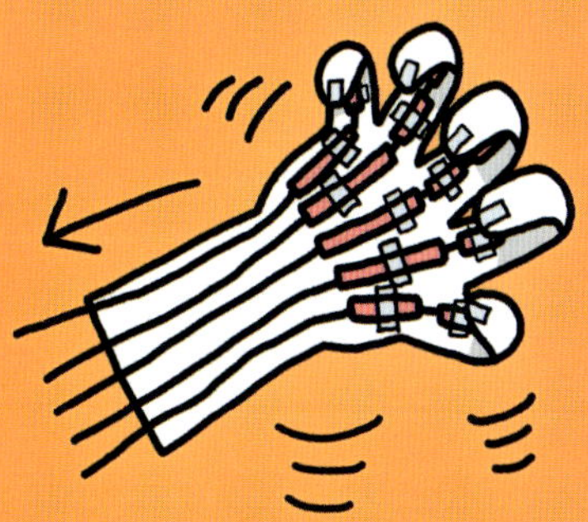

5. Find the line of straws that runs from the wrist to the top of the thumb. Thread a piece of string through it and tape down at the top.

6. Repeat with the fingers. Pull on each string to move the fingers. Can you use the strings to hold up one finger? Three fingers? Make a fist?

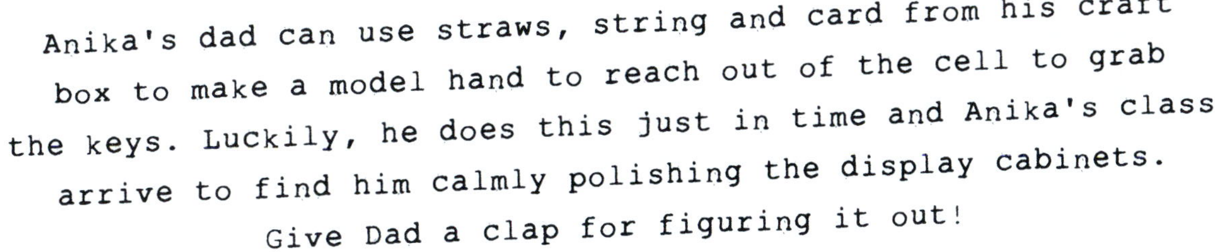

Anika's dad can use straws, string and card from his craft box to make a model hand to reach out of the cell to grab the keys. Luckily, he does this just in time and Anika's class arrive to find him calmly polishing the display cabinets. Give Dad a clap for figuring it out!

CALAMITY COMICS

8

# HOW TO SOLVE THE CASE OF THE VANISHING VEGGIES

THE SCIENCE COMIC YOU NEVER KNEW YOU NEEDED | BIOLOGY EDITION

Archie's grandad has been off adventuring in his new spaceship. He's just got home and brought some new friends with him – aliens! Luckily, they don't want to take over the planet. They love gardening and spend their time growing asparagus. When it's in season there's nothing yummier!

But their asparagus has disappeared!

The alien's first suspect was Grandad's cat, Gus – but he HATES asparagus.

Now there are three suspects left: Grandad, his neighbour Fran and the postie. How can the aliens solve the mystery?

Should the alien crew . . .

A) USE THEIR NOSES?

B) DUST FOR FINGERPRINTS?

C) FORCE SOMEONE TO CONFESS?

If you chose **A**, YES! You got it. When asparagus is eaten it gives your pee a very distinct whiff. Luckily, these aliens have a powerful sense of smell. If they put it to good use, they'll catch the culprit in no time!

If you chose **B**, oh dear. Grandad has just finished his weekly deep clean.

If you chose **C**, oops. The postie cracks first - but it wasn't her. She doesn't even like asparagus! Now the aliens might never get their parcels delivered on time.

## WHAT'S THE SCIENCE?

We have five main senses: smell, sight, touch, taste and hearing. It's how we experience the world (and know that eating a freshly baked biscuit is scrumptious).

But how do we smell things? Well, it involves the nose and the brain. There are around 10 million tiny smell receptors in the nose! Each one detects a different type of smell. When the receptors pick up on a smell, they send a message to the brain via neurons so it can figure out what the smell is. Being able to tell the difference between smells also helps with being able to tell the difference between tastes.

Let's have a go at a super sniffing experiment.

# TEST YOUR SMELL POWERS

Luckily, we don't have to sniff pee in this experiment - yuck! Let's use tomato juice instead to put your nose to the test!

## You will need:

- Seven clear cups
- A marker pen
- Seven sticky labels
- Water
- A metal spoon
- One tablespoon of tomato juice
- A blindfold
- A friend

## Instructions:

1. Fill the cups halfway with water. Write the numbers 1–7 on the sticky labels and put one on each cup.

2. Mix the tomato juice into cup 1.

3. Mix a spoonful of liquid from cup 1 into cup 2.

4. Mix a spoonful of liquid from cup 2 into cup 3.

5. Keep going until you have mixed a spoonful from cup 5 into cup 6. Don't add anything to cup 7.

6. Shuffle the cups so they aren't in order. Take turns with your friend to wear the blindfold and sniff the cups. Can either of you guess the numbers correctly?

If the aliens are quick, they can get to the bathrooms of all the suspects. There, they can use their powerful noses to sniff out the asparagus-muncher from the smell of their pee. Mission accomplished - and it was Grandad who was the sneaky veg thief!

CALAMITY COMICS

9

# HOW TO AVOID A TURTLE MELTDOWN

*THE SCIENCE COMIC YOU NEVER KNEW YOU NEEDED* BIOLOGY EDITION

Wei and his little sister Mimi are at a family outing to the zoo. Mimi **LOVES** turtles and is desperate to go and see them – but the turtle enclosure shuts early today! And they are still busy looking at the lions with their cousin.

One of the zoo staff is telling them about what lions eat . . .

. . . and what their poo looks like!

Wei and Mimi's cousin says he can't believe that the lion cub can create that huge pile.

Mimi isn't going anywhere until their cousin understands how the lion's poo was made. What can Wei do to help?

Should Wei . . .

A) GET HIS LUNCHBOX?

B) DRAW MIMI A TURTLE?

C) SUGGEST SEEING THE KOALAS INSTEAD?

If you chose **A**, GREAT idea! Wei can use some crackers, water and orange juice to show their cousin how food turns into poo.
If you chose **B**, Mimi isn't impressed. Day trip disaster!
If you chose **C**, this doesn't work. It's turtles that Mimi wants to see!

## WHAT'S THE SCIENCE?

After your teeth have chomped up your food, it travels down a tube in your throat called the **oesophagus** – about ten seconds later it lands in your stomach, a bit like a slide.

The stomach contains acid, which helps break down the food into a soft, partially digested mixture called **chyme**. The chyme then goes into the 8-metre-long **intestines**. First, in the small intestine, **enzymes** help the body absorb the nutrients it needs to work well. Then, water is removed from the liquidy chyme in the last part of the large intestine, leaving the stuff we don't need as faeces (poo!). This is stored in the rectum (part of the large intestine), before it's released into the toilet.

Let's have a closer look at how digestion works with an experiment.

# SEE DIGESTION IN ACTION

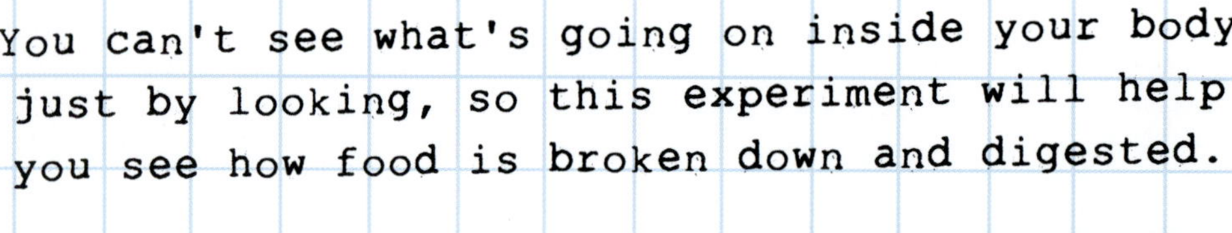

You can't see what's going on inside your body just by looking, so this experiment will help you see how food is broken down and digested.

**You will need:**

- A resealable sandwich bag
- Three crackers
- One tablespoon of water
- One tablespoon of orange juice
- Scissors*

*Be careful – ask an adult for help.

**The whole process of human digestion takes around 24–72 hours – lions can take longer to digest their food. This is because in the wild they eat much larger meals, less frequently. Their digestive systems are adapted for eating large amounts of meat in one go!**

**Instructions:**

1. Place the crackers in the sandwich bag and seal it tight.

2. Break up the crackers into little pieces. This is like teeth crunching food. Be careful – don't tear the bag.

3. Add the water. This will work like saliva! Seal the bag and shake to mix.

4. Open the bag and add the orange juice (this works like the acid and enzymes in the stomach. You can also use vinegar – a stronger acid – to see more of a change).

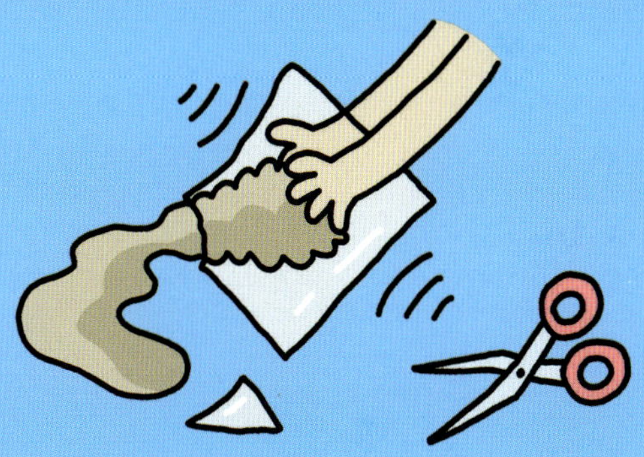

5. With the bag fully sealed, knead the mixture together.

6. Ask an adult to snip off the corner. Squeeze out the mixture. The crackers should look nothing like the ones you'd put cheese on!

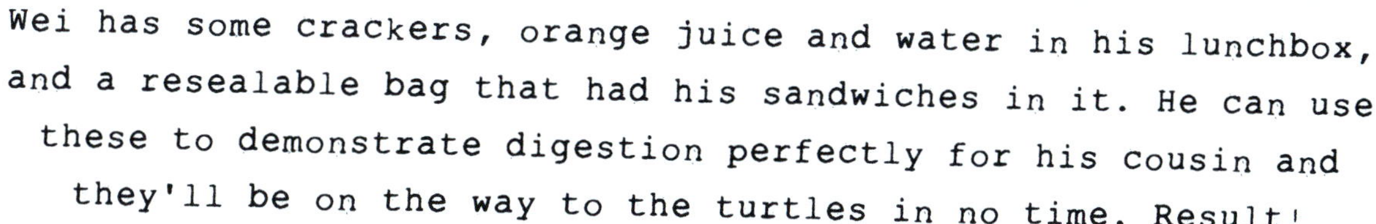

Wei has some crackers, orange juice and water in his lunchbox, and a resealable bag that had his sandwiches in it. He can use these to demonstrate digestion perfectly for his cousin and they'll be on the way to the turtles in no time. Result!

CALAMITY COMICS

10

# HOW TO MAKE AN INTERGALACTIC LUNCHBOX

*THE SCIENCE COMIC YOU NEVER KNEW YOU NEEDED* | BIOLOGY EDITION

Amy's granny is going to be the FIRST GRANNY IN SPACE! She's got her spacesuit, she's done her training and now she's heading to the rocket for lift-off. On the mission, Granny has been put in charge of bringing lunch for everyone.

She had planned a delicious salad . . .

. . . but she's left her bag of vegetables at home!

It was a looooong flight and now Granny is on Mars, she's a bit peckish . . . and she's only brought food to last for a few weeks!

Should Granny . . .

A) TRY TO CALL FOR A TAKEAWAY?

B) ASK THE NEIGHBOURS FOR A SNACK?

C) HAVE A FEEL OF THE SOIL ON MARS?

If you chose **A**, sadly Granny's phone has run out of battery.
If you chose **B**, oh no. The locals don't know what a snack is!
If you chose **C**, GREAT IDEA! Since Mars has water (mostly as ice), light and carbon dioxide, and Granny's crew have built a special growing pod, she can grow her own edible garden.

# WHAT'S THE SCIENCE?

To grow into a plant, seeds need somewhere warm, ideally deep in soil, with lots of water to drink. Happy in its bed, a plant will grow roots and sprout stems. This is called **germination**.

On Earth, there is plenty of light, water and carbon dioxide – three key ingredients for healthy plants to grow, using a process called photosynthesis. On Mars, though, it is colder and darker, so plants would need to be grown in special chambers (buildings that keep plants warm and well-lit). The soil on Mars is also different, so would need treating. Scientists think that the **nutrients** in astronauts' pee and poo might help plants to grow in this soil! Maybe Granny could give it a go . . .

Are you ready to try growing your own plants? No poo or pee needed!

# MAKE A SEED BOMB

Don't worry, there's no need to get on a flight to Mars to grow your own garden. Here on Earth we have the perfect conditions to help seeds blossom into plants!

## You will need:

- A mixing bowl
- A handful of compost
- Clay powder (about half as much as the compost)
- A packet of lettuce leaf seeds
- Water
- A spoon
- Paper towels

**Compost is a brilliant fertiliser made of decomposing material such as food ... and poo! It provides nutrients for the seeds in these little 'bombs', and the water is a refreshing drink to help them sprout roots and stems.**

## Instructions:

1. Put the compost, clay powder and a spoonful of seeds into the mixing bowl. Give the mixture a stir to combine.

2. Slowly mix in the water and stir with the spoon. Stop adding water as soon as everything in the bowl starts to stick together.

3. Shape the mixture into balls and put them on top of the paper towels to dry. The dry clay and compost mix gives the seeds some protection from hungry animals.

4. Throw your seed bombs in your garden (check with an adult first). Watch over the next few weeks to see if they grow. If you don't have a garden, you could ask a friend, family member or a neighbour if you could use theirs.

Luckily, Granny went to the garden centre recently and she's got some tomato, potato and carrot seeds in her handbag – all plants that scientists have grown in Mars-like soil. She wouldn't be able to just throw her seeds outside . . . but with the help of the space crew on Mars and their special growing chamber, Granny can plant her veg seeds and fill up the crews' lunchboxes, no problem.

**Fertiliser has lots of nutrients that help plants grow. You can make fertiliser from eggshells for plants that like calcium-rich soil. Just ask an adult to wash the eggshells, grind them up and then mix with the soil.**

# CALAMITY COMICS

11

# HOW TO WIN A PIRATE SAILING RACE

*THE SCIENCE COMIC YOU NEVER KNEW YOU NEEDED* | *BIOLOGY EDITION*

Mo, his aunty and his best friend Wei have entered the biggest pirate sailing race! Their boat is super speedy and they can't wait to celebrate on the beach afterwards. The only problem is Captain Rottenleg and his scurvy crew have turned up to race too!

They've been neck and neck for the whole race and now it's the final stretch.

Captain Rottenleg will do anything to win . . .

. . . including cannonballing a hole in Mo's boat!

Water is coming in fast . . . what can they do to get them over the finish line before they sink?

Should Mo and his crew . . .

A) JUMP OVERBOARD?

B) PANIC?

C) GRAB THEIR INFLATABLE FLAMINGO?

If you chose **A**, oops. Now they've lost the race AND are soaking wet! If you chose **B**, oh dear, panicking never works . . . everyone needs to take lots of deep breaths to calm down. If you chose **C**, GREAT PLAN! They can use the air inside their inflatable to help push the boat to victory.

# WHAT'S THE SCIENCE?

The solution is all about air! We inhale (breathe in) oxygen from the air every few seconds. Oxygen is essential for many living things, including humans, to convert food into energy. When we inhale, oxygen enters the lungs and crosses the cell membranes into the blood. At the same time, carbon dioxide (a waste gas made by the cells) moves from the blood into the lungs. Exhaling gets rid of the carbon dioxide.

Muscles are also important for breathing. When you breathe in, your rib muscles pull your ribcage outwards and your diaphragm (a muscle at the bottom of your chest) moves downwards to draw in the air. When you breathe out, these muscles relax, pushing the waste gases out of your lungs.

Turn the page to find out how the science of breathing and air could help win the race!

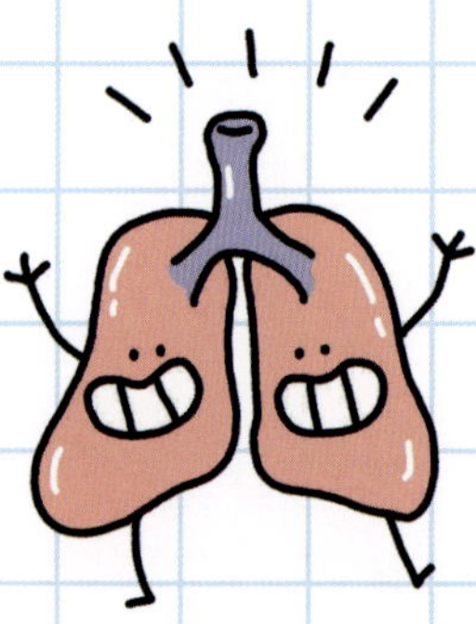

# MAKE YOUR OWN LUNGS

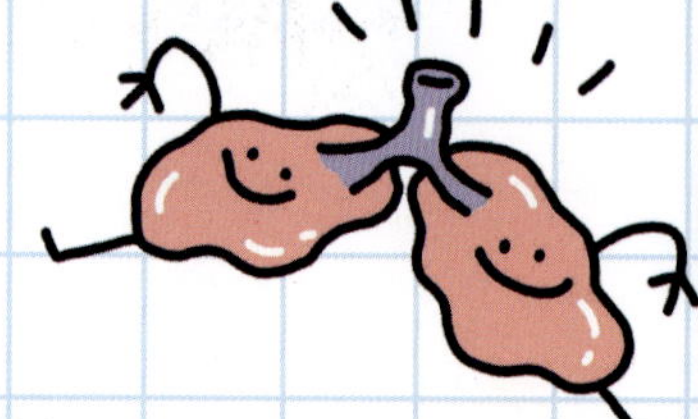

You can think of lungs like balloons – they become rounder when air goes into them and flatter when air goes out. Here's a fun way of showing the process of breathing.

**The left lung is smaller than the right lung because it has to share space with the heart.**

## You will need:

- A small plastic bottle
- Scissors*
- Two balloons
- Sticky tape

*Be careful – ask an adult for help.

## Instructions:

1. Ask an adult to help you cut off the bottom of the plastic bottle. Be careful of the sharp edge!

2. Push the balloon inside the bottle's neck, leaving the opening coming out of the top.

3. Pull the balloon's opening around the outside of the bottle's neck and secure with sticky tape.

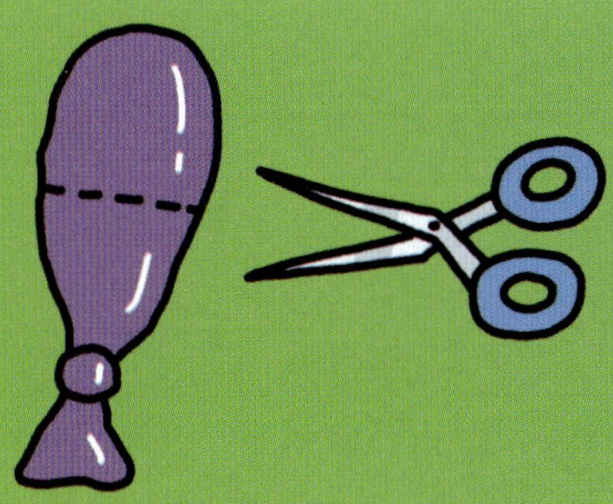

4. Ask an adult to knot the other balloon and cut it in half across the middle.

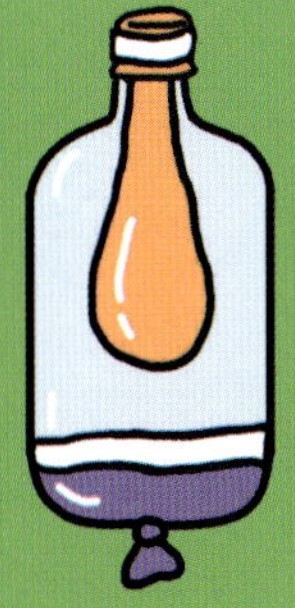

5. Ask an adult to help you stretch the knotted half around the other end of the bottle. Tape in place if needed.

6. Pull down on the knot. What does this do to the balloon inside the bottle?

**The diaphragm moves down when we inhale, drawing air into the lungs. Similarly, pulling down on the knotted balloon makes more space in the bottle. Air is drawn into the top balloon to fill the space, like air fills our lungs.**

Air rushing out of the lungs can create a pressure that can move objects – try blowing on a page of this book to see for yourself! If Wei takes the stopper out of the inflatable, the air rushing out could help push the boat forwards. True, it would need to be a VERY big inflatable to push out enough air . . . but if it was large enough, and Mo pointed the air away from the boat, they might just win!

CALAMITY COMICS

12

# HOW TO TURN CELERY INTO MAGIC RAINBOW FLOWERS

*THE SCIENCE COMIC YOU NEVER KNEW YOU NEEDED* | *BIOLOGY EDITION*

It's Mother's Day tomorrow and Rocky and Flynn have both completely forgotten. Again. And Dad's only gone and made Mum a gigantic bouquet of her favourite mini cereal boxes!

Last year, Rocky and Flynn gave her a half-eaten sandwich from Rocky's lunchbox . . .

. . . so she has high expectations of better gifts this year.

Panicked, Rocky and Flynn look around for inspiration.

Will a bouquet of celery impress their Mum?

Should Rocky and Flynn . . .

A) PANIC AND MAKE UP A RAP?

B) MAGIC THE CELERY INTO FLOWERS?

C) PRETEND THEY MADE DAD'S BOUQUET?

If you chose **A**, uh oh. Rocky and Flynn are terrible at rapping. All they can think of to rhyme with 'Mum' is 'bum'. Mum is not impressed.

If you chose **B**, FANTASTIC IDEA. They don't even need a magic spell - they can use the magic of SCIENCE instead!

If you chose **C**, Dad is not happy. He spent all night gluing boxes of cereal together and he tells on the boys straight away.

## WHAT'S THE SCIENCE?

The plant 'magic' here is caused by photosynthesis - the process that all green plants use to make their food. Leaves capture light from the Sun - they also have tiny holes on their underside called stomata, that take in carbon dioxide. Water from the ground travels up through the roots. Some water escapes from the stomata when the plant collects carbon dioxide, in a process called **transpiration**. The water travels upwards through tiny tubes called capillaries - a process called capillary action.

Knowing how water travels through a plant will help Rocky and Flynn create an exciting-looking bouquet for Mum. Ready to have a go too?

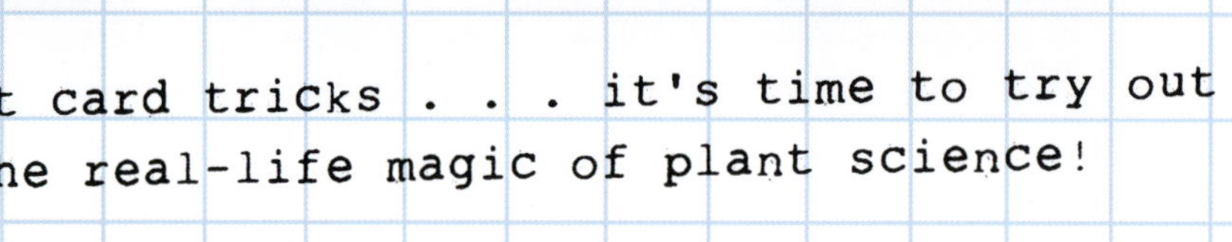

# MAKE A RAINBOW BOUQUET FROM YOUR FRIDGE DRAWER

Forget card tricks . . . it's time to try out the real-life magic of plant science!

## You will need:

- Four glasses
- Water (room temperature)
- Food colouring (four different colours)
- A teaspoon
- Four sticks of celery with leafy tops
- Scissors*
- A ruler

*Be careful – ask an adult for help.

## Instructions:

1. Fill each glass about half full with water.

2. Stir 3-4 drops of food colouring into each glass with the spoon. Put a different colour in each one. (If you only have one colour, put the same in all four glasses.)

3. Ask an adult to cut approximately two centimetres off the bottom of each stem (measure with the ruler).

4. Place one stick of celery in each glass. Leave overnight.

5. In the morning you'll be able to see that the tops have changed colour!

**After you have left the stems overnight, tear them open to see how the colour has moved up. Remember not to eat the celery once it has changed colour!**

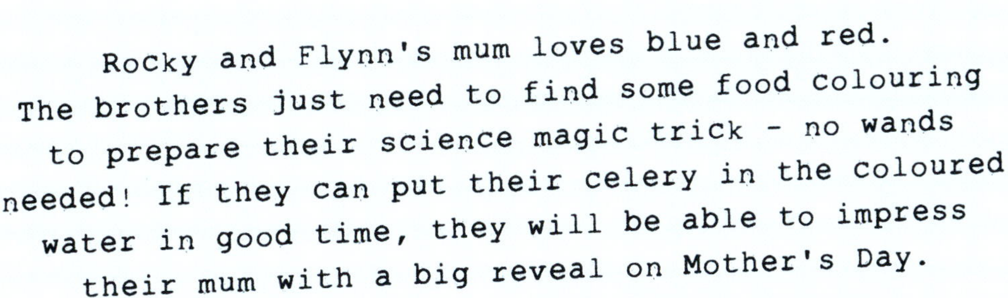

Rocky and Flynn's mum loves blue and red. The brothers just need to find some food colouring to prepare their science magic trick - no wands needed! If they can put their celery in the coloured water in good time, they will be able to impress their mum with a big reveal on Mother's Day.

**CALAMITY COMICS** **13**

# HOW TO STOP A T. REX FROM EATING YOUR SOCKS

*THE SCIENCE COMIC YOU NEVER KNEW YOU NEEDED* — BIOLOGY EDITION

Archie's grandad turned up with an egg from his most recent expedition. What he wasn't expecting was for it to hatch . . . into a baby T. rex!

Archie has named him Brian. They WERE getting on fine . . .

. . . but then Brian decided that Archie's socks were PERFECT for munching.

If Archie wants to save his lucky football socks, he needs a plan.

And fast!

Should Archie . . .

C) DISTRACT BRIAN BY DANCING?

B) HIDE HIS SOCKS?

A) HEAD TO THE PARK WITH GRANDAD?

If you chose **A**, this is a nightmare. Brian is laser-focused on snacks and will not be distracted.

If you chose **B**, disaster. Archie's sock camouflage skills are no match for Brian's brilliant eyesight.

If you chose **C**, BRILLIANT IDEA! The park near Archie's house is full of animals. By watching them, he can gather information that might help.

## WHAT'S THE SCIENCE?

All animals, including humans, need food to survive. We also need air, water and shelter in our **environment**. How long do you think a person could manage without any of these things? Half a day? A few hours? A few minutes?

All are essential, though animals can go different lengths of time without them. For example, humans can live for about two months without food if they had to, but just a few days without water (don't try this at home!).

Animals have lots of ways of meeting their needs - such as building homes to stay warm, or foraging for food. Some animals even travel long distances to find food and water at different times.

Turn the page to get up close with animals finding food and shelter in their surroundings . . .

# MAKE A WORM FARM

Earthworms work hard underground to find food and water, and make a comfortable home. Let's watch them in action!

## You will need:

- A large, clear plastic bottle
- Soil (two-three handfuls)
- Sand (two-three handfuls)
- Fruit/veg peelings (one handful)
- Leaves (one handful)
- Water
- Three earthworms*
- Plastic wrap
- An elastic band
- A sharp pencil**
- Black paper
- Scissors**
- Sticky tape

*Handle earthworms very carefully – and wash your hands afterwards.

**Be careful – ask an adult for help.

## Instructions:

1. Ask an adult to cut off the top of the bottle. Fill it with alternating layers of soil, sand and peelings, ending with a layer of soil.

2. Water until moist (not soaking wet) and place a layer of leaves on top.

3. Add your earthworms and cover the top with plastic wrap. Secure with the elastic band and ask an adult to pierce some air holes with a pencil.

4. Wrap the bottle in black paper, secure with tape and leave it in a cool place. Take off the plastic wrap and add a little water each day to keep it moist.

5. After a week, take the paper off. Have any of the peelings been eaten? You may see tunnels where the earthworms have moved through the layers.

**The bottle acts like the earthworms' underground home. The peelings, leaves and soil provide food, and wrapping the bottle in black paper makes it dark, like the earthworms are used to.**

In the park, Archie will be able to see animals looking for food – maybe even an earthworm! Observing the animals will help Archie work out that Brian's sock-eating is because he's HUNGRY. Getting him some dinosaur food will protect Archie's football socks from being chomped up. Maybe Grandad can help by telling Archie what food there was on his expedition – hopefully Brian is a plant eater . . .

# GLOSSARY

**ATOMS:** The tiny building blocks that make up everything in the Universe.

**AUXIN:** A hormone (a chemical) in plants that helps them grow towards light.

**CARBON DIOXIDE:** A gas made of carbon and oxygen atoms.

**CELL MEMBRANES:** The outer layer of cells.

**CHYME:** A liquidy mixture of partially digested food.

**ENVIRONMENT:** Everything that surrounds us.

**ENZYMES:** Tiny chemical substances in the body that help with digestion.

**GERMINATION:** The stage when a seed starts to grow.

**INTESTINES:** Long tubes, including the small and large intestines, where food is digested.

**JOINTS:** Areas in the body where two or more bones meet.

**MUSCLES:** Soft tissues that connect the bones and help the body move.

**NEURONS:** Cells that carry information from the brain around the body.

**NUTRIENTS:** Important substances that help living things (including humans and plants) to grow.

**OESOPHAGUS:** The tube that carries food from the mouth to the stomach.

**PHOTOSYNTHESIS:** The process that plants use to make their own food.

**PULSE:** The beat of your heart, which can be felt in different places in your body, such as your wrist.

**ROOTS:** The parts of plants that grow underground.

**SKELETON:** All the bones that make up the body's frame.

**TRANSPIRATION:** The process where water is pulled up through the plant from the roots.

# INDEX